Workbook for
Dr. Mindy Pelz's
Fast Like a Girl

By Brighter Health Publishing

Published by Brighter Health Publishing

ISBN: 9798856774428

Printed in the United States of America

We give, verbatim, the same disclaimer that Mindy Pelz and her publisher offer in the book *Fast Like a Girl*:

This book contains general information and advice relating to the potential benefits of fasting. It is not intended to replace personalized medical advice. As with any new health protocol, the practices recommended in this book should be followed only after consulting with your doctor to make sure they are appropriate to your individual circumstances. The author and publisher expressly disclaim responsibility for any adverse effects that may result from the use or application of the information contained in this book.

Table of Contents

Part I: The Science

Chapter 1: It's Not Your Fault

The human body functions as a well-coordinated team of cells, requiring proper nutrients to perform optimally. In her book *Fast Like a Girl*, Mindy Pelz highlights the failure of trendy diets that disregard the body's natural design, leading to health issues, and emphasizes the importance of understanding and embracing a new health paradigm that aligns with the body's needs for sustainable results.

Mindy Pelz encourages the reader to release guilt and shame associated with past dieting failures and assures them that they are not alone in their struggles and presents alarming statistics about women's health issues and further emphasizing the need to forgive oneself and let go of negative thoughts in order to embark on a healing journey towards reclaiming power and achieving better health.

Here are five important diet failures that Pelz lays out in this chapter:

1: Counting Calories Does Not Work

The text debunks the myth that counting calories leads to permanent weight loss and highlights the negative effects of calorie-restriction diets on the body's metabolic set point. It explains how the body adapts to lower calorie intake by increasing hunger signals and slowing down metabolism, making it difficult to sustain weight loss. The Minnesota Starvation Experiment is cited as evidence of the physical and mental health consequences of long-term calorie restriction.

2: Beware Poor Food Quality Choices

Four decades ago, the American government's anti-fat stance led to the rise of low-fat foods, which replaced fat with sugar and chemicals, contributing to the obesity epidemic. These ultra-processed foods cause insulin resistance, where cells can't effectively use insulin to process glucose, leading to energy depletion and fat storage. Insulin resistance is a root cause of metabolic syndrome, and diets that fail to address this issue are bound to be unsuccessful in achieving lasting results.

3: Watch Out for Cortisol Spikes

Cortisol, the stress hormone, negatively impacts insulin and hinders health. Calorie-restriction diets and rigid eating plans can induce stress, leading to cortisol spikes that disrupt digestion, fat burning, and increase glucose levels. Cortisol can also rise due to overexercising or daily stresses, affecting hormonal balance and insulin levels. Sustained stress undermines health regardless of diet or exercise efforts.

4: Limit Exposure to Toxic Ingredients

Toxins known as obesogens can contribute to weight gain by being stored as fat in the body. Chemicals such as BPA plastics, phthalates, atrazine, organotins, and PFOA are considered obesogens, and are commonly found in food, water, beauty products, and more. These obesogens can block hormonal receptor sites, interfering with the proper functioning of hormones and leading to weight gain, fatigue, and other health issues. Detoxing these chemicals from the body can help address weight-loss resistance, thyroid problems, and autoimmune conditions. Awareness of ingredient labels and avoiding foods and drinks, including water, with obesogens is crucial for a healthier approach.

5: There Is No One-size-fits-all Approach

In this book, Mindy Pelz emphasizes that there is no one-size-fits-all diet, particularly for women who have different hormonal needs throughout their lives. The harmful belief that all women should follow the same diet has led to suboptimal health outcomes. Hormones such as estrogen and progesterone have distinct food requirements, and diets should be adjusted accordingly. Additionally, exposure to obesogens can disrupt hormonal receptors and lead to weight gain, fatigue, and other health issues. The focus on one-size-fits-all approaches in diets overlooks the importance of accommodating individual hormone needs, whether for cycling women or postmenopausal women.

Fast Like a Girl encourages women to approach their relationship with food by adapting their diets to their menstrual cycles, a skill that should have been taught since puberty and modified throughout menopause. By tuning lifestyle needs to the monthly cycle, hormonal issues like infertility and polycystic ovary syndrome can be alleviated. The destructive nature of comparison with other women, based on their diet results, is highlighted, emphasizing the importance of finding a customized diet tailored to one's own hormones. The book urges readers to recognize the power within their own bodies and explore the unique path to health, syncing lifestyle choices with hormones for effortless well-being. The inward journey of fasting is presented as a means of unlocking the body's self-healing mechanisms, such as autophagy, when combined with mindful food choices.

Mindy Pelz describes the story of a YouTube subscriber named Sarah who struggled with weight gain despite following calorie-cutting and low-fat diets recommended by doctors. Frustrated, she turned to YouTube and discovered fasting videos that resonated with her. She immersed herself in learning about fasting and customized it to her unique needs, resulting in significant weight loss and improved health. This story emphasizes the power and potential of women to find their own unique path to health by syncing lifestyle choices with hormones.

Mindy Pelz concludes this chapter by urging readers to let go of past failures, reject the five diet failures, and embrace a new vision of health, setting the stage for an exciting journey.

Chapter 2: The Healing Power of Fasting

Our hunter-gatherer ancestors experienced cycles of fasting and feasting, which scientists believe shaped our genetic coding to adapt to these periods. The "thrifty gene" hypothesis suggests that our health suffers when we deviate from this ancestral feast-famine pattern, contributing to the rise in rates of obesity and diabetes. Examples like Ramadan fasting demonstrate the positive effects of extended periods without food. By studying the Muslim community during Ramadan, valuable research on fasting has been conducted. Looking back in history, these instances provide evidence of the human body thriving in a fasted state.

Fasting has a significant impact on our genetic code and healing mechanisms, as scientific research confirms. In this chapter, we will explore the modern-day concept of fasting, the activation of healing processes, and the potential benefits for women when engaging in longer fasts. To understand fasting, we must first recognize the two fuel systems our cells rely on: sugar and fat. When we eat, our cells utilize glucose as fuel in the sugar-burner energy system. However, during fasting, our cells transition to the fat-burner system, akin to a hybrid car switching to electric power. This shift typically occurs around eight hours after the last meal.

Intermittent fasting, as supported by a comprehensive analysis published in The New England Journal of Medicine, offers numerous healing benefits for various conditions such as obesity, diabetes, cardiovascular disease, neurodegenerative brain conditions, and cancer. This approach triggers essential cellular responses including increased ketones, mitochondrial stress resistance, antioxidant defenses, autophagy, and DNA repair, while decreasing glycogen, insulin, mTOR, and protein synthesis. Research suggests that changing when you eat, rather than just what you eat, is crucial for metabolic health improvement. Studies demonstrate that condensing the eating window and allowing for longer fasting periods leads to reduced body fat, waist circumference, blood pressure, LDL cholesterol, and hemoglobin A1c levels.

Research demonstrating the importance of changing the time period in which we eat rather than the quality of food gives hope for reversing metabolic damage and improving overall health. Intermittent fasting, a simple practice that involves compressing the eating period, yields incredible results without the need for dietary changes or significant resources. By accessing the fat-burning state through fasting, not only can weight loss, blood pressure, cholesterol, and insulin levels be improved, but the body also undergoes deep healing, similar to the restorative effects of sleep. Fasting is a gift that allows the body and brain to recover from the stresses of modern life and is distinct from other diets.

Some important benefits of fasting include:

Fasting Increases Ketone Levels:

Ketones are produced by the liver when blood sugar levels drop, serving as an alternative fuel source for cells in the absence of glucose. They possess healing properties, particularly in repairing nervous tissue and regenerating damaged neurons, leading to improved memory, focus, and mental clarity. Ketones also energize mitochondria, reset their function, and provide consistent energy throughout the day. Additionally, ketones suppress hunger hormones, induce a calming effect, and contribute to a sense of limitlessness and increased healing with fasting.

Fasting Increases Autophagy:

Autophagy is a powerful cellular process that kicks in during a fasted state, improving cellular resilience through detox, repair, and the removal of diseased cells. This self-eating mechanism was discovered by Nobel laureate Dr. Yoshinori Ohsumi, and its benefits are profound, revitalizing cells and promoting a youthful and vibrant feeling. Autophagy plays a crucial role in priming the immune system to fight viruses, as it deprives them of energy and inhibits replication. Additionally, autophagy removes worn-out cellular parts, repairs mitochondria, and eliminates malfunctioning cells, offering a comprehensive approach to building high-performing cells and preventing disease. By combining autophagy with ketosis through fasting, the body enters an amplified healing state, unlocking its full potential.

Fasting Decreases Glycogen and Insulin Stores:

If you've been consuming a high-sugar diet, your body stores the excess sugar as glycogen in muscles, liver, and fat. Fasting allows your body to tap into these glycogen stores and use them for fuel, helping to undo the damage caused by previous diets and resulting in lasting weight loss. Fasting also leads to the release of excess insulin stored in the liver and fat, reversing insulin resistance. By changing when you eat and compressing your food intake into a shorter period, around 8 to 10 hours, you can achieve optimal metabolic health without the need to drastically alter your diet, offering a transformative approach to weight loss and improved well-being.

Fasting Increases Growth Hormone Production:

As we age, the production of growth hormone declines, leading to various signs of aging. Growth hormone plays a crucial role in burning fat, promoting muscle growth, and supporting brain function. Fasting can stimulate the production of growth hormone, helping to burn fat, increase muscle size, and enhance cognitive abilities, providing a youthful boost to our bodies and minds.

Fasting Resets Dopamine Pathways:

Frequent eating and indulging in delicious food raise our dopamine baseline, leading to a need for more dopamine to feel satisfied. This can result in dopamine resistance, similar to insulin resistance, where obese individuals require more food to experience a normal dopamine response. However, fasting can reset dopamine pathways, preventing the decline of dopamine receptors and increasing their sensitivity, ultimately promoting feelings of contentment and satisfaction.

Fasting Repairs the Immune System:

Fasting, particularly a three-day water fast, has remarkable effects on the immune system. In patients undergoing chemotherapy, fasting triggers the release of stem cells into the bloodstream, resulting in the elimination of old, worn-out white blood cells and the generation of new, energized ones. This immune system reboot is vital for individuals undergoing chemotherapy. Additionally, fasting has the potential to reset dopamine pathways, reducing dopamine resistance and increasing sensitivity, thereby enhancing feelings of contentment and satisfaction.

Fasting Improves Your Microbiome:

Fasting has a significant impact on our microbiome, which consists of trillions of bacteria that play a crucial role in supporting our overall health. Modern lifestyles, including diet, medication use, stress, and exposure to Wi-Fi, are detrimental to our beneficial microbes. However, fasting can help restore the health of our microbiome by improving microbial diversity, moving microbes away from the gut lining, increasing the production of bacteria that convert white fat to brown fat (which is easier to burn), and regenerating intestinal stem cells. Fasting has also been shown to positively influence blood pressure and can be more effective in promoting changes than dietary modifications alone.

Fasting Reduces the Reoccurrence of Cancer

Fasting for 13 hours or more has been shown to reduce the risk of breast cancer recurrence by 64% due to the significant decrease in blood glucose levels and inflammation. This finding highlights the incredible potential of fasting as a powerful tool for health. Additionally, the story of a patient named Lani who defied a three-month prognosis for metastatic breast cancer by exploring various healing approaches emphasizes the importance of prevention through daily commitment to fasting. These findings offer hope that fasting can be a valuable strategy in the fight against cancer, and further studies continue to emerge supporting its benefits.

Six different fast lengths

The six different types of fast are:

1. Intermittent fasting: 12–16 hours
2. Autophagy fasting: starts at 17 hours
3. Gut-reset fast: 24 hours
4. Fat-burner fast: 36 hours
5. Dopamine-reset fast: 48 hours
6. Immune-reset fast: more than 72 hours

Intermittent Fasting:

Intermittent fasting is the most popular style of fasting, typically involving 12 to 16 hours without food. During this fasting period, your body transitions into a state of ketosis, where it burns fat for energy and produces ketones. This leads to benefits such as reduced hunger, increased physical and mental energy, cellular repair, detoxification, and improved metabolic markers. Intermittent fasting is an effective approach for weight loss, combating brain fog, and addressing energy loss, making it a suitable option for those seeking these specific outcomes.

Autophagy:

Autophagy, a cellular healing process, gradually increases around 17 hours of fasting and reaches its peak at 72 hours. Extending your fast beyond this point can trigger autophagy and provide various benefits, including detoxification, improved brain function, prevention of colds, and balanced sex hormones.

Gut Reset:

The gut reset fast is a favorite choice due to its ease, time efficiency, and significant impact on the microbiome. Fasting for 24 hours or more triggers the release of stem cells that repair the damaged mucosal lining of the gut affected by chronic inflammation. This fast is particularly effective in improving gut health, supporting the immune system, and addressing issues like antibiotic use, birth control use, and small intestinal bacterial overgrowth (SIBO).

Fat Burner:

Fasting has gained popularity for its effective weight-loss benefits, but some people who fast daily still struggle to lose weight. Leading women through 36-hour fasts proved to be a successful approach, activating a fat-burning switch that shorter fasts couldn't achieve. Incorporating occasional 36-hour fasts can help minimize weight-loss resistance, release stored sugar, and reduce cholesterol levels.

Dopamine Fast:

Fasting for 48 hours can provide a mental health boost by repairing dopamine receptor sites and improving dopamine pathways. Participating in Fast Training Week, where the community practices fasting for different lengths of time, has shown that the 48-hour dopamine fast has the most significant impact on mental health. This length of fast helps reboot dopamine levels and lower anxiety levels, with the benefits becoming more noticeable in the weeks following the fast.

Immune Reset:

The three-to-five-day water fast, also known as an extended fast, is beneficial for stem cell regeneration. After 72 hours of fasting, the body produces revitalized stem cells that can heal aging cells and address chronic conditions. Extending the fast to five-plus days further maximizes stem cell production and can help ease chronic conditions, prevent disease, alleviate musculoskeletal pain, and slow down the effects of aging.

Chapter 3: Metabolic Switching: the Key to Weight Loss

Your body has the incredible ability to regenerate itself, with different body parts replacing cells at varying rates. However, diseased cells can replicate and contribute to aging and symptoms. By practicing metabolic switching through fasting, which involves shifting from glucose to ketones for energy, you can promote healing and repair in your cells. Metabolic switching benefits various aspects of your health, including liver and gut repair, brain neuron restoration, and overall cellular rejuvenation. Mimicking the feast-famine cycle of our primal ancestors can provide opportunities for metabolic switching and improve your chances of optimal health and survival.

Alternating between autophagy and mTOR

Metabolic switching involves alternating between two cellular processes, autophagy and mTOR, which are responsible for cellular breakdown and growth respectively. Constantly stimulating mTOR through continuous eating accelerates aging, while excessive autophagy from excessive fasting can break down skeletal muscle. However, incorporating periods of fasting and feeding allows you to benefit from both pathways, promoting cellular rejuvenation and growth when done in moderation. Metabolic switching can be especially beneficial for women when timed with their menstrual cycle, supporting weight loss, muscle building, and hormonal production.

Creating a hormetic stress

Metabolic switching creates a hormetic stress on the body, promoting cellular adaptation and improved efficiency, similar to the effects of varying workouts to continuously challenge the body for better results. When transitioning from frequent eating to intermittent fasting, the initial shift induces a healing state and yields positive outcomes, but to sustain the benefits, it is necessary to vary the lengths of fasts and maintain the hormetic stress on cells for ongoing metabolic strength.

Healing your mitochondria

Metabolic switching has a profound impact on mitochondria, which are responsible for energy production and cellular detoxification. By utilizing both glucose and ketones as fuel sources, metabolic switching improves mitochondrial efficiency, enhancing energy levels and preventing fatigue. Additionally, healthy mitochondria produce glutathione and control methylation, essential for reducing oxidative stress, inflammation, and toxin removal, ultimately restoring cellular health and promoting overall well-being.

Regenerating neurons in your brain

Metabolic switching repairs and grows neurons in your brain, enhancing mental cognition and preventing neurodegeneration, while also providing numerous health benefits such as slowing aging, promoting weight loss, boosting memory, balancing the gut, preventing cancer, detoxifying the body, and alleviating autoimmune conditions.

The four of of these work together to slow aging, help with weight loss, improve memory, balance the gut, keep away cancer, mobilize toxins, and alleviate autoimmune disorders.

Chapter 4: Fasting a Woman's Way

Bridget, a high-tech executive, experienced weight gain and health issues despite her exercise routine, leading her to try intermittent fasting. Initially successful, she later faced adverse symptoms such as heart palpitations, anxiety, and hair loss, prompting her to consult a doctor who advised against fasting. After discovering gender-specific fasting approaches, she adjusted her regimen to match her hormonal fluctuations, resulting in improvements in hair loss, anxiety, and sleep. Understanding the menstrual cycle's impact on hormones and aligning lifestyle habits accordingly can optimize women's health and well-being.

Your menstrual cycle:

Days 1-10

During the menstrual cycle, estrogen gradually increases from its lowest levels at the start until reaching a peak around mid-ovulation, providing benefits such as improved skin elasticity, stronger bones, and enhanced mood and mental clarity, as estrogen contributes to the production of collagen and acts as a precursor to neurotransmitters that promote calmness and happiness.

Days 11-15

During days 11-15 of the menstrual cycle, the ovulation period, estrogen and testosterone play a significant role, with estrogen providing physical and mental benefits and testosterone giving a sense of power, strength, motivation, drive, and energy, making it an ideal time for starting new projects, taking on challenging tasks, and engaging in strength-training workouts.

Days 16-18

During this stage, all of your hormones decrease, resembling the first week of your cycle, but with the shift of your body focusing on progesterone production instead of estrogen, you may experience a decline in energy and mental clarity.

Days 19-Bleed

During the last stage of your menstrual cycle, the production of progesterone increases, bringing a sense of calmness, reduced aggression, and a desire to relax. Maintaining low cortisol levels during this phase is crucial for optimal progesterone levels, as cortisol can interfere with its production, leading to symptoms like missed cycles and irritability. Additionally, it's important to be mindful of glucose and insulin levels, as progesterone requires sufficient glucose while estrogen is negatively affected by high glucose and insulin.

Why we need to fast differently:

Women's hormonal cycles are longer and much complicated than men's. For these reasons, we must adjust the way we approach intermittent fasting.

The power of our hormonal hierarchy

The hormonal hierarchy principle explains that oxytocin can calm cortisol, and cortisol spikes can lead to increased insulin levels, which in turn affect sex hormones. The hypothalamus and pituitary glands work together to balance hormones, with the hypothalamus receiving hormonal signals and instructing the pituitary gland to produce specific hormones. When cortisol signals are received, a cascade of events occurs, involving glucose metabolism and insulin release from the pancreas.

Insulin

Insulin surges signal the hypothalamus to inhibit the production of estrogen and progesterone, as the body prioritizes dealing with the ongoing crisis over reproductive functions, highlighting the hierarchy of hormonal responses. However, by targeting oxytocin at the top of the hormonal chain, the brain can suppress cortisol, leading to improved glucose management, reduced insulin levels, and a restoration of sex hormone balance, bringing the entire system back into equilibrium.

Cortisol

Managing stress is a challenging task, as cortisol can wreak havoc on both mental and physical well-being, but understanding the impact of cortisol on hormonal health can motivate positive change. Chronic stress leads to cortisol spikes, which increase blood sugar levels and trigger insulin production, hindering weight loss efforts and disrupting sex hormone balance. However, fasting like a girl can help counteract the negative effects of cortisol, while oxytocin, the top hormone in the hierarchy, has the power to restore hormonal balance and combat chronic stress.

Oxytocin

Increasing oxytocin levels leads to a drop in cortisol, resulting in balanced insulin levels and improved sex hormone production. Activities that promote oxytocin release, such as hugging, laughing, expressing love, and engaging in meaningful connections, should not be underestimated as they are essential for women's well-being and can bring hormonal harmony by influencing the hypothalamus and halting cortisol production. Prioritizing daily doses of oxytocin can have significant health benefits.

Fluctuations in our sex hormones

Women commonly experience fluctuations in appetite and cravings throughout their menstrual cycle, often attributing them to lack of willpower or discipline, when in fact they are influenced by the interplay of insulin and cortisol with different sex hormones, making fasting easier or more challenging at various times during the month.

Estrogen

Estrogen benefits from fasting, particularly in the early phase of the menstrual cycle, as it thrives when insulin levels are low, and the interplay between estrogen and insulin can be disrupted in menopause and perimenopause, leading to weight gain and hormonal imbalances.

Testosterone

Intermittent fasting can increase testosterone levels in men, but its effect on women is not well-studied. Based on clinical experience, it is recommended for women to limit fasting to a maximum of 15 hours during ovulation when estrogen and testosterone are at their peak, as prolonged fasting may negatively impact hormone balance. Cortisol, a stress hormone, can decrease testosterone and progesterone, so caution should be exercised in undertaking longer fasts during this time.

Progesterone

The week before your period, when your body is producing progesterone, is a crucial time to avoid fasting due to progesterone's susceptibility to cortisol and glucose, as activities that raise cortisol or lower glucose levels can negatively impact progesterone levels, making fasts of any length unfavorable during this phase.

The impact of our toxic loads

Toxins can affect hormones by acting as endocrine disruptors, leading to chronic diseases. Hormonal surges, particularly of estrogen and progesterone, can also trigger the release of stored toxins in the body. During these surges, longer fasts that stimulate autophagy can result in a double dose of toxins being released, causing detox symptoms. It is important for women to modify their fasting routine according to their monthly cycle to avoid negative hormonal consequences and customize a fasting lifestyle that suits their bodies.

Part II: The Art of Fasting Like a Girl

Chapter 5: Build a Fasting Lifestyle Unique to You

Build a Fasting Lifestyle Unique to You

The emergence of personalized health care, also known as functional medicine, has challenged the one-size-fits-all approach of conventional medicine. This approach focuses on understanding individual health conditions and collaborating with patients, as seen in the successful n-of-1 trials, empowering them to take control of their well-being and customize their fasting lifestyle based on their unique needs and circumstances.

The Four Pillars of a Fasting Lifestyle

Pillar 1: Identify Your Fasting Goals

Lose Weight

When building a fasting lifestyle, it's important to acknowledge that women tend to lose weight differently from men, and incorporating occasional longer fasts, like 36-hour fasts, can significantly accelerate weight-loss results for women if timed correctly in their menstrual cycle.

Balance Hormones

Many women have found fasting beneficial for hormonal conditions like PCOS, infertility, and menopause symptoms, as regulating insulin through fasting can naturally balance sex hormones. To optimize fasting for hormonal balance, follow outlined protocols for specific conditions and consider getting a hormonal test to tailor fasts accordingly to address imbalances effectively.

Alleviate Specific Conditions

Fasting can be highly beneficial for women dealing with various challenges like autoimmune conditions, cancer, diabetes, mood disorders, dementia, or Alzheimer's. Specific protocols are outlined in the appendix of this book.

Pillar 2: Vary Your Fasting Lengths

The fasting goal is to establish a personalized pattern that suits you effortlessly as a sustainable health habit. After finding your initial fasting window, the next step is to incorporate fasting variation, which prevents plateaus, aligns with hormonal surges, and offers flexibility in your fasting routine.

Honor Your Hormones

Women's bodies require varying fasts to align with hormonal fluctuations, and following the Fasting Cycle, adjusting fasts to match hormonal surges, leads to effortless fasting. Adverse fasting reactions occur when not tuned to menstrual variation, but by honoring estrogen and progesterone needs during peak and low hormone levels, respectively, optimal fasting results can be achieved.

Avoid Plateaus

By varying your fasting lengths, you will avoid the weight loss plateaus associated with restrictive diets. Your body needs change in order to jumpstart the healing benefits of fasting.

Stay Flexible

The beauty of varying your fasts lies in its flexibility, allowing you to easily adapt to changes in your routine, vacations, holidays, and social gatherings. Fasting offers freedom and the ability to create a personalized fasting lifestyle that fits seamlessly into your life experiences.

Pillar 3: Vary Your Food Choices

Variety in food choices is essential for optimizing your feminine body's health. Overcoming cravings and diversifying your food intake through ketobiotic and hormone feasting can positively influence your gut microbiome, ultimately leading to improved long-term health and reduced cravings. Building a fasting lifestyle, along with varying both fasts and foods, is a powerful way to change cravings and enhance overall well-being.

Pillar 4: Surround Yourself With a Supportive Community

Having a supportive community is crucial for success in any diet regimen, as positive connections boost oxytocin, influencing hormonal balance and amplifying results. Surrounding yourself with supportive friends, exercising together, and sharing experiences can make the healing journey enjoyable and effective for everyone involved.

Lifestyle Considerations

Relationships

The importance of positive and supportive relationships for a healthy life is paramount. Fasting like a girl offers flexibility to ensure you can still enjoy meals with loved ones while thriving with your health, making it customizable and adaptable to family demands.

Schedule

Varying your fasts and food allows you to adapt your fasting lifestyle to any circumstance. For example, actress Kat Graham faced a challenging schedule during a nighttime movie shoot, so implementing short intermittent fasts with coffee and MCT oil until early evening boosted her energy and helped her through the filming process.

Activity level

Adapting your fasting lifestyle to match your activity level is crucial for optimal performance. Customizing fasting and eating windows based on energy demands and hormonal fluctuations can significantly enhance stamina and overall performance, ensuring a personalized and joyful approach to life's endeavors.

Chapter 6: Food That Supports Your Hormones

Food Principle 1: Ingredients Matter

Reading food labels and scrutinizing the ingredients is vital for hormonal health. Opting for foods with healthy, recognizable ingredients while avoiding chemically-laden options is crucial in supporting hormone production and preventing metabolic disease. Remember, the length and familiarity of the ingredient list are essential factors to consider when making food choices.

Toxic Ingredients to Avoid

Today, food companies prioritize shelf life and profits over consumer health, resulting in an increase in toxic ingredients in our foods. The GRAS (generally recognized as safe) category allows for potentially harmful ingredients to be added without rigorous testing, raising concerns among consumer protection groups. It's essential to be cautious of unfamiliar or hard-to-pronounce ingredients and be aware of seemingly harmless ones, like "natural flavorings," which may still be harmful.

Choose foods that resemble nature rather than those created in a chemistry lab for optimal hormone health. Whole, natural foods like fresh potatoes are more nutritious than processed options like potato chips.

Foods to Add

Your sex hormones (estrogen, progesterone, and testosterone) are affected by your diet, and understanding their preferences can be advantageous for hormonal balance. Estrogen thrives with a low-carbohydrate diet and benefits from good fats, cholesterol-rich foods, and healthy phytoestrogens like organic soy, seeds, nuts, legumes, fruits, and vegetables. By supporting healthy estrogen production, you can address imbalances and promote hormonal health.

Foods That Support Estrogen

GOOD FATS

- Olive oil
- Flaxseed oil
- Sesame seed oil
- Avocados

SEEDS AND NUTS

- Brazil nuts
- Almonds
- Cashews
- Roasted salted peanuts
- Pine nuts
- Pumpkin seeds
- Sunflower seeds
- Walnuts
- Sesame seeds

LEGUMES

- Peas
- Chickpeas
- Soybeans
- Lima beans
- Carob
- Kidney beans
- Mung beans
- Pinto beans
- Black-eyed peas
- Lentils

FRUITS AND VEGETABLES

- Sprouts
- Cabbage
- Spinach
- Onion
- Garlic
- Zucchini
- Broccoli
- Cauliflower
- Strawberries
- Blueberries
- Cranberries

Foods That Support Progesterone

Progesterone, like estrogen, is influenced by your food choices but has different preferences. While estrogen thrives with low blood sugar, progesterone benefits from slightly higher blood sugar levels. Before your period, you may naturally crave carbohydrates as your body prepares to produce progesterone. Foods supporting progesterone production tend to be higher on the glycemic index, like potatoes, but avoid harmful oils to prevent inflammation.

ROOT VEGETABLES

- White potatoes
- Red potatoes
- Sweet potatoes
- Yams
- Beets
- Turnips
- Pumpkin
- Butternut squash

CRUCIFEROUS VEGETABLES

- Brussels sprouts
- Cauliflower
- Broccoli

TROPICAL FRUITS

- Bananas
- Mangoes
- Papaya

CITRUS FRUITS

- Oranges
- Grapefruit
- Lemons

SEEDS

- Sunflower
- Flax
- Sesame

LEGUMES

- Chickpeas
- Kidney beans
- Black beans

Muscle Building Foods

Building muscle is vital for overall health, as it improves metabolism, bone strength, mental health, and longevity. Fasting leans you out, while eating protein stimulates muscle growth through mTOR activation. Choosing the right protein involves considering quality and quantity, with animal protein providing all nine essential amino acids for muscle building, while plant-based proteins require a variety of sources to complete the amino acid profile. For muscle growth, focus on leucine-rich foods like animal-based proteins and certain plant sources or consider amino acid supplements if needed.

- Chicken
- Beef
- Pork
- Fish
- Milk
- Cheese
- Eggs
- Tofu
- Navy beans
- Pumpkin seeds

Microbiome Supporting Foods

Focus on probiotic-rich foods to support the diverse bacterial population in your gut. Antibiotics, stress, and other factors can deplete beneficial microbes, but adding fermented foods, such as kimchi, can quickly replenish them. Fermented foods offer various health benefits, including improved digestion, increased vitamins and minerals, enhanced mental health, and strengthened immunity, with each food providing unique healing effects.

PROBIOTIC-RICH FERMENTED FOODS

- Sauerkraut
- Kimchi
- Pickles
- Yogurt
- Kefir dairy
- Kefir water
- Kombucha

To nourish the good bacteria in your gut, focus on prebiotic-rich foods, which act as fuel for these beneficial microbes. Just as you would feed and care for a beloved pet, providing prebiotics supports a healthy microbiome. Some powerful prebiotic foods, resembling hormone-building foods, are particularly beneficial for women's health.

PREBIOTIC RICH FOODS

- Chicory root
- Dandelion root
- Konjac root
- Burdock root
- Onions
- Jerusalem artichoke
- Garlic
- Leeks
- Asparagus
- Red kidney beans
- Chickpeas
- Split peas
- Cashews
- Pistachios
- Hummus

To support a healthy gut, incorporate polyphenol-rich foods, such as red wine and dark chocolate, into your diet. These antioxidants create a nurturing environment for diverse gut microbes to thrive. Quality matters, so choose natural, low-alcohol wines and dark chocolate with high cacao content and minimal sugar. Polyphenol-dense foods offer various health benefits, including regulating blood pressure, improving circulation, reducing inflammation, and protecting against neurodegenerative diseases. Many polyphenol foods are plant-based, and herbs and spices are also rich sources of polyphenols.

POLYPHENOL RICH FOODS

- Artichoke hearts
- Broccoli
- Brussels sprouts
- Cloves
- Saffron
- Oregano
- Rosemary
- Thyme
- Basil
- Cinnamon
- Cumin
- Curry

- Dark chocolate
- Olives
- Parsley
- Red wine
- Shallots

Food Principle #2 Glycemic Load Matters

Monitoring blood sugar is a crucial indicator of overall health, with abnormal levels possibly indicating metabolic disease. The glycemic index ranks foods based on their impact on blood sugar, and choosing foods with a low glycemic index helps reduce glucose and insulin, making fasting easier and promoting fat-burning energy. Understanding macronutrients and their effect on blood sugar is essential for metabolic health and can lead to increased energy, weight loss, and improved mental clarity.

Carbohydrates

Carbohydrates can be classified as simple or complex based on their impact on blood sugar. Simple carbohydrates cause rapid spikes in blood sugar and can lead to storage of excess glucose as fat, while complex carbohydrates with more fiber have a slower impact on blood sugar and support overall health. Nature-made complex carbohydrates are preferable, while processed simple carbohydrates (such as cookies, crackers, cereals, chips, breads, pastas, and the majority of processed foods) can contribute to obesity and other health issues.

When measuring macros for fasting like a girl, focus on net carbohydrates (total carbs minus fiber). Fiber in foods slows sugar absorption, while simple carbohydrates raise blood sugar quickly. Nature-made complex carbs are recommended for better compatibility with our bodies.

Protein

Protein has a positive effect on blood sugar by breaking down slowly, slowing carb absorption, and reducing hunger. Favoring protein over simple carbs can help with fasting. Limit protein intake to around 75 grams per day to avoid excessive blood sugar spikes.

Fat

Fat stabilizes blood sugar, kills hunger, and plays a crucial role in cellular health. Embrace good fats that nourish your cells and avoid bad fats that cause inflammation. The importance of healthy fats is gaining recognition, and they are making a comeback in the nutritional world.

Food Principle #3 Diversity Matters

Diverse food choices are crucial for nurturing a healthy gut microbiome. Different foods feed different gut bacteria, and increasing variety in your diet can promote the growth of beneficial microbes. Aim for 200 different types of complex carbohydrates, proteins, and fats in your diet each month to support microbial fitness and maintain a happy gut. Some spices to add more diversity into your diet are:

- Cardamom
- Cumin
- Celery seed
- Onion powder
- Garlic powder
- Star anise
- Black pepper
- Turmeric
- Rosemary
- Thyme
- Basil
- Saffron
- Nutmeg
- Allspice
- Cloves
- Cinnamon

Food Principle #4 Cycling Matters

Cycling your food choices with your hormonal patterns can optimize your health and hormone balance. By following the Fasting Cycle or the 30-Day Fasting Reset, you can align your food and fasting with your menstrual cycle or hormonal fluctuations. Understanding and embracing this approach will magnify the power of your hormones and make the process enjoyable and empowering.

Putting It All together

Using these food principles, we can create a functional diet using two different modes of eating. As you cycle between ketobiotic and hormone feasting diets, your sex hormones will be supported throughout your cycle.

Ketobiotic

Women need to approach the ketogenic diet differently, as they require more carbs and protein to support their sex hormones. The ketobiotic diet combines the benefits of low-carb living with a focus on plant-based foods to optimize blood sugar, fat burning, and estrogen production. The key rules are limiting net carbs to 50g, consuming natural carbohydrates from vegetables and greens, keeping protein intake below 75g, and making good fats more than 60% of the diet.

The ketobiotic diet offers several benefits for women. It aids in weight loss by promoting quick fat-burning and supports optimal estrogen production. Additionally, it provides essential nutrients for the liver and gut, vital for detoxifying harmful estrogens, and triggers the release of healing ketones that benefit the hormonal control center in the brain.

Hormone Feasting

Hormone feasting days are designed to support progesterone production in women by providing higher carbohydrate intake. These days intentionally increase blood glucose levels and may take you out of ketosis to promote progesterone production. The rules include consuming up to 150 grams of net carbs, focusing on natural carbohydrates like root vegetables and fruits, limiting protein to 50 grams, and enjoying healthy fats as desired.

Chapter 7: The Fasting Cycle

How the Fasting Cycle Works

The Fasting Cycle divides the menstrual cycle into three phases: Power, Manifestation, and Nurture, each focused on specific hormones. It's designed for a 30-day period, but can be adjusted to fit individual cycle lengths. Experiment with fasting and food options to find what suits you best, and consider using the 30-Day Fasting Reset for structure. Longer fasts can be beneficial when timed appropriately for your cycle, promoting a hormetic response and healing.

The Power Phases (Days 1–10 and 16–19)

- Suggested fasting lengths: 13–72 hours
- Optional food style: ketobiotic
- Hormone focus: insulin, estrogen
- Healing focus: autophagy and ketosis

The Fasting Cycle has two "Power Phases" (days 1-10 and days 16-19) when aggressive fasting (longer than 17 hours) is beneficial due to low hormone levels. These phases are ideal for triggering autophagy and ketosis, repairing brain and ovarian cells, and improving hormone production. Ketobiotic eating, focusing on low carbs and high good fats, complements the fasts during these phases, while fruits and starches are reserved for "Hormone Feasting Days."

The Manifestation Phase (Days 11–15)

- Suggested fasting length: <15 hours
- Optional eating style: hormone feasting foods
- Hormone focus: estrogen, testosterone
- Healing focus: supporting a healthy gut and liver

During the manifestation phase, characterized by high estrogen, testosterone, and a mild surge of progesterone, women feel their best and experience hormonal bliss. This phase focuses on metabolizing hormones through liver and gut support, especially for detoxifying estrogen to prevent hormonal imbalances and related health issues. Leaning into hormone feasting foods during this period helps nourish the liver and gut, aiding in proper digestion and nutrient absorption.

During the manifestation phase, it's best to keep fasts under 15 hours to avoid potential detox reactions from hormone surges. This phase is characterized by a significant testosterone surge, which can be optimized by reducing exposure to toxins and stressors. Phthalates, for example, can disrupt testosterone production and should be avoided. Focusing on hormone feasting foods and minimizing fasting duration can lead to a more comfortable and thriving experience during this period.

Avoiding phthalates found in plastics and personal care products with strong fragrances is essential for overall hormonal health, especially for optimizing testosterone levels. Stress during the manifestation phase can suppress progesterone and testosterone production, as cortisol production takes priority, leading to symptoms like low libido, motivation, and increased anxiety. Monitoring DHEA levels through hormone tests can provide valuable insights into the impact of stress on these crucial hormones.

The Nurture Phase (Day 20–First Day of Your Period)

- Suggested fasting length: no fasting
- Optional eating style: hormone feasting foods
- Hormone focus: cortisol, progesterone
- Healing focus: reducing cortisol

The nurture phase is the time to focus on yourself and nurture your body. Skipping fasting and engaging in nurturing activities like yoga or hiking is recommended during this phase. Emphasize hormone feasting foods, including starchy options like potatoes and squashes, as your body becomes more insulin resistant during this time, requiring more glucose to produce progesterone and promote a sense of calm.

The Fasting Cycle as Lifestyle

Whether you're new to fasting or have experience, the Fasting Cycle offers a helpful approach to time your fasts appropriately. The 30-Day Fasting Reset provides a proven plan tailored to your menstrual cycle or life stage, allowing you to optimize your hormones. Remember, your body is designed to self-heal, and as you experience the benefits of fasting, you'll likely be motivated to explore longer fasts. Embrace this journey and let your body's natural healing abilities guide you.

Part III: The 30-Day Fasting Reset

Chapter 8: The 30-Day Fasting Reset

Metabolically Flexing to Satisfy All Your Hormones

For this 30-day reset, you'll focus on three different-length fasts ranging from 13 to 20 hours to create a healing effect. If you're new to fasting, the two-week pre-reset work will help ease your experience. Embrace the uncomfortable moments during the reset, as they lead to healing through hormesis. Plan ahead for potential obstacles like hunger, boredom, detox symptoms, or lack of support, and refer to Chapter 10 for effective strategies to navigate them.

Timing Your Fasts to Your Cycle

This reset follows the phases of the Fasting Cycle, including no fasting, intermittent fasting, autophagy fasting, and a gut-reset fast, all timed to your cycle. If you have a cycle, track it and start the reset on day one of your next period. If you don't have a cycle, start anytime and follow the 30-day reset. This approach can help balance hormones and address various hormonal imbalances, even leading to a return of menstrual cycles for some women or relief from postmenopausal symptoms.

Resets Done in a Community

Health endeavors are most successful when supported by a team of cheerleaders, and as women, connection is vital for us. Positive relationships have a significant impact on health and happiness, as shown in the Harvard University 80-year study, where those with warm relationships lived longer and happier lives. Building a community around you, such as joining a book club or online fasting community, can provide essential human connection for a great hormonal boost during your health journey.

Who Is This Reset For?

All women can benefit from this fasting reset. It can help alleviate the symptoms of the following:

- Weight-loss resistance
- Insulin resistance
- Diabetes
- Prediabetes
- Cardiovascular conditions
- Autoimmune conditions
- Memory problems
- Mood disorders such as anxiety and depression
- Hormonal cancers

- Infertility challenges
- Gut dysbiosis
- Menopause symptoms
- Brain fog
- Low energy
- Missed cycles
- Detoxing from birth control
- Repairing your gut post antibiotic use
- Lack of motivation
- Hair loss
- Thyroid challenges
- Accelerated aging

Pre-reset: Two Weeks Leading up to Your 30 Day Fasting Reset

If you're new to fasting, don't worry—this pre-reset is for you. It's designed to prepare your body for the fasting experience by easing you into lifestyle changes. The two-week pre-reset involves avoiding certain foods, adding in specific foods, and compressing your eating window to help your blood sugar stabilize and make fasting easier. Taking your time and following the pre-reset will set you up for success with your new fasting lifestyle.

Foods to Avoid During the Pre-reset:

HARMFUL OILS:

- Partially hydrogenated oils
- Corn oil
- Cottonseed oil
- Canola oil
- Vegetable oil
- Soybean oil
- Safflower oil
- Sunflower oil

REFINED SUGAR AND FLOUR:

- Breads
- Pastas
- Crackers
- Desserts

SYNTHETIC INGREDIENT:

- Artificial colors and flavorings
- Red or blue dyes

- Saccharin
- NutraSweet
- Splenda

Foods to Add:

As you remove harmful foods from your diet, you may experience increased cravings due to changes in gut microbes and blood sugar fluctuations. Stabilizing blood sugar and hunger hormones by adding more good fats and protein can help stop these cravings.

GOOD FATS TO ADD:

- Olive oil
- Avocado oil
- MCT oil
- Flaxseed oil
- Pumpkin seed oil
- Grass-fed butter
- Nut butters
- Olives
- Avocados

HEALTHY PROTEIN TO ADD:

- Grass-fed beef
- Turkey
- Chicken
- Pork
- Eggs
- Charcuterie meats like salami and prosciutto

Compressing Your Eating Window

During the two-week pre-reset, gradually compress your eating window by pushing breakfast back an hour every two days until you can fast for 13 hours. Coffee and tea with a small amount of MCT oil and clean cream can help kill hunger and support the fasting process. After completing the pre-reset, you are ready to begin the 30-day fasting reset.

Tips for Succeeding at Your Reset

For newcomers to fasting, the two-week pre-reset is recommended to ease into the 30-day reset. Remove tempting foods from your home and surround yourself with supportive, positive people to cheer you on during this journey. Be cautious of food buddies who may inadvertently hinder your progress, and encourage them to join you or understand your commitment to the reset.

The 30 Day Fasting Reset

Overview:

Foods to Avoid:

- Bad oils
- Refined flours and sugar
- Toxic chemical ingredients
- Alcohol

Food Styles:

- Ketobiotic
- Hormone feasting

Types of Fasting:

- Intermittent fasting (13 hours and 15 hours)
- Autophagy fasting (17 hours)

POWER PHASE 1

- Food choice throughout the phase: ketobiotic
- Days 1–4: intermittent fasting (13 hours)
- Day 5: intermittent fasting (15 hours)
- Days 6–10: autophagy fasting (17 hours)

MANIFESTATION PHASE

- Food choice throughout the phase: hormone feasting foods
- Days 11–15: intermittent fasting (13 hours)

POWER PHASE 2

- Food choice throughout the phase: ketobiotic
- Days 16–19: intermittent fasting (15 hours)

NURTURE PHASE

- Food choice throughout the phase: hormone feasting
- Days 20–30: no fasting

Advanced Fasting Reset

If you already have experience with fasting, try this advanced fasting reset. The option to fast the week before your period assumes that a 13 hour fast will not spike your cortisol levels because of your previous fasting experience.

POWER PHASE 1: -Ketobiotic Foods

- Days 1–5: intermittent fasting (15 hours)
- Day 6: gut-reset fast (24 hours)
- Days 7–10: autophagy fasting (17 hours)

MANIFESTATION PHASE: -Hormone Feasting Foods

- Days 11–15: intermittent fasting (15 hours)

POWER PHASE 2: -Ketobiotic Foods

- Day 16: gut-reset fast (24 hours)
- Days 17–19: autophagy fasting (17 hours)

NURTURE PHASE: -Hormone Feasting Foods

- Days 20–30: intermittent fasting (13 hours)

Tools to keep you on track:

Monitoring your body's biometrics during the fasting reset can be beneficial for your success. Blood sugar and ketone readings can be measured using a glucose monitor. Morning readings help you assess your fasting state, while pre-meal and post-meal readings provide insights into fat-burning and insulin sensitivity. These measurements can be more motivating and informative than relying solely on the scale.

In the morning (before coffee) take a blood sugar reading. Ideally your blood sugar should be in between 70–90 mg/dL (milligrams per deciliter). Your ketones will likely be low in the morning around .2 mmol/L. Right before you break your fast take another reading: you want your blood sugar to be lower and your ketones higher than they were first thing in the morning. If this is the case, you an be sure that your body is transitioning to a fat burning mode. Lastly, take a blood sugar measurement two hours after eating. If your blood sugar is back down close to the pre-meal measurement than your body is insulin sensitive. This is a great thing! If it hasn't moved back down, don't worry. The more you fast the more insulin sensitive you will become.

Chapter 9: How to Break a Fast

Fasting is not as simple as some may think, and properly breaking a fast is equally important. The author has found four ways to approach breaking a fast based on health goals, and the strategy depends on desired outcomes. Research on food intake after fasting has been limited, prompting the author to conduct their own research with the community to determine the best approaches.

Reset Your Microbiome

Fasting promotes microbiome repair, and breaking your fast with probiotic-rich foods, prebiotic foods, and polyphenol foods can further support beneficial gut bacteria. Recommended foods for breaking a fast include fermented yogurts (dairy or coconut-based), bone broth, sauerkraut, and kombucha. Combining these options can be beneficial for your gut health.

Build More Muscle

Fasting does not break down muscles; the temporary shrinkage is due to sugar release from muscles. Breaking your fast with a protein-rich meal, such as bone broth, eggs, or a plant-based protein shake, can help build muscles stronger, especially when combined with strength training in a fasted state. Eating periodic doses of 30 grams of protein throughout the day is an efficient way to stimulate muscle growth.

Post-Fasting Foods for Supporting Muscle Growth:

- Eggs
- Beef sticks
- Beef jerky
- Protein shakes such as pea, hemp, and whey concentrate
- Sliced deli meats (nitrite-free)
- Chicken breast
- Turkey
- Grass-fed beef
- High-protein vegetables such as peas, broccoli, sprouts, mushrooms, and brussels sprouts
- Chickpeas
- Lima beans
- Quinoa
- Avocado

Follow Your Taste Buds

Breaking a fast with a poor food choice won't undo the healing effects of fasting, but it's better to be intentional with what you eat. Following your taste buds may provide instant satisfaction, but other methods are better for your health. A daily fasting regime of 14 to 16 hours can undo metabolic damage caused by a poor diet, but specific health goals may require more attention to food choices and blood sugar regulation. Understanding the nuances of breaking a fast is crucial for successful fasting.

What Pulls You out of a Fasted State?

In the fasting window, some drinks may not raise blood sugar and won't break the fast for certain individuals. However, it varies based on personal factors such as microbiome diversity and insulin resistance. Customizing fasting according to these variables is crucial for individual success. Common fasting-friendly drinks include coffee, tea, and mineral water, but testing is essential to determine their impact on blood sugar.

Poor Microbial Diversity

The diversity of your gut microbiome significantly influences how your blood sugar responds to food and drinks. A healthy and diverse microbiome leads to better blood sugar management. Gut microbes have a direct connection to the liver, and in a fasted state, they signal the liver to switch to the fat-burning energy system. Repairing your microbiome can improve your blood sugar regulation and fasting experience.

Insulin Resistance

Insulin resistance can cause blood sugar spikes even with minimal drinks. It's essential to recognize the varying degrees of insulin resistance, which can affect fasting results. Understanding these factors helps determine the best approach during fasting.

In general, certain drinks may break a fast, while others are less likely to do so. Drinks like coffee creamers, sweeteners, sodas, diet drinks, Gatorade, and alcohol may disrupt fasting. On the other hand, supplements, medications, black coffee, coffee with full-fat milk, tea, oils (e.g., flaxseed and MCT), and mineral water are usually considered acceptable during fasting.

Fasted Snack

Fasted snacks can be consumed during fasting without breaking it, helping to extend fasting windows and aid in weight loss. Some suitable options include nut butter, bone broth, or coffee with full-fat cream and butter. However, fasted snacks should only be used temporarily and stopped once they are no longer needed during longer fasts. Recommended fasted snacks include ¼ cup of grass-fed cream, 1 tablespoon of MCT oil, 2 tablespoons of nut butter, or 1 tablespoon of seed oil.

Breaking a Longer Fast

For shorter fasts (less than 48 hours), use the strategies mentioned above. For longer fasts (48 hours or more), follow a four-step process for refeeding: start with broth, eat a probiotic-rich meal with fat, steam veggies, and finally, include animal protein. This gradual approach helps reintroduce food strategically and maintain the healing effects of the fast.

Chapter 10: Hacks That Make Fasting Effortless

Handling Hunger While Fasting

Learn to differentiate between true hunger and boredom. Engage in mood-lifting activities to distract yourself from food cravings. If hunger persists, try mineral packets like LMNT or Redmond to address potential mineral imbalances and satisfy your taste buds without breaking your fast.

If still hungry, consider a fasted snack like a small fat bomb (e.g., full-fat cream and MCT oil in coffee or tea) to extend your fasting window. Test the snack's impact on your blood sugar to ensure it works for you. Another hack is feeding your gut microbes in a fasted state by adding a prebiotic powder like inulin to your drinks, helping to curb hunger signals from your gut.

Coffee and tea can be beneficial during fasting, but it's essential to test their impact on your blood sugar as individual reactions may vary. Ensure your coffee is mold- and pesticide-free to avoid potential blood sugar spikes. Look for "organic" or "mold-free" labels on coffee packaging or inquire with the company for purity assurance. Avoid coffee with chemicals that may contribute to insulin resistance.

Experiencing the keto flu when entering ketosis is common and may include symptoms like rashes, fevers, muscle aches, constipation, brain fog, and fatigue. These symptoms are signs of the body healing and detoxifying. To alleviate detox symptoms, vary your fasts and ensure your detox pathways, including liver, gut, kidneys, lymph, and skin, are open for effective toxin elimination.

Tips for Aiding Detoxification

Daily dry brushing with a hard brush exfoliates the skin and opens pores for toxin elimination. Sweating helps in detoxification by promoting circulation and opening pores. Additionally, lymphatic massage aids in moving toxins away from organs, preventing detox reactions. Using a rebounder trampoline promotes lymph flow, aiding in detoxification. An Epsom salt bath with warm water and magnesium helps extract toxins from the skin, alleviating detox symptoms. Additionally, using binders like zeolite or activated charcoal can help remove environmental toxins and heavy metals released during autophagy.

Measuring Blood Sugar and Ketones

Measuring your blood sugar and ketones is optional, but it can provide valuable insights into your fasting lifestyle. Check your levels in the morning and before your first meal, aiming for blood sugar between 70-90 mg/dL and ketones above 0.5 mmol/L. Avoid using urine measurements and breathalyzers, as they are not accurate. Instead, use a blood sugar and ketone meter or a continuous glucose monitor (CGM) for more precise and continuous readings. CGMs offer real-time data on how your body responds to different foods and fasts, helping you optimize your fasting routine.

Strategies for Getting your Blood Sugar to Decrease

Hack 1: Fast Longer

If fasting isn't producing the desired blood sugar results, consider trying longer fasts, like a 36-hour fat-burner fast. Giving your body more time to adapt to fasting and experience hormetic stress can help switch it into fat-burning mode. Be patient and let your body find its optimal metabolic state through experimentation with fasting principles.

Hack 2: Vary Your Fasts

Variation is essential to keep your body adapting positively. Like when the pandemic disrupted routines, initially leading to a blissful experience but later causing agitation, sticking to the same fasting pattern can halt your progress. To prevent this, try different fasting methods, including days without fasting, to enhance your body's metabolic flexibility and avoid plateaus.

Hack 3: Avoid All Processed Foods

Processed foods contain chemicals that wreak havoc on our blood sugar. If you are not noticing results from fasting, consider cutting out ALL processed foods until your body can get things under control.

Hack 4: Love Your Liver

Your liver plays a crucial role in entering ketosis, but it may need support to function optimally. Minimize liver-loading habits like drug and alcohol use, as they can hinder ketosis. Implement liver hacks like castor oil packs, coffee enemas, infrared saunas, essential oils, bitter lettuces, and dandelion tea to ensure a healthy liver and improve your fasting lifestyle.

Hack 5: Support Your Adrenals

When struggling to enter ketosis, adrenal fatigue could be a factor affecting blood sugar regulation. Adrenals work in tandem with the brain, and symptoms like dizziness when standing up and salt cravings may indicate adrenal challenges. A DUTCH hormone test can provide insights, and supplementation can be used to support the adrenals.

Hack 6: Remove Toxins

If other methods are not effective, consider detoxifying to remove long-standing toxins like heavy metals, which can impact the liver, cell mitochondria, and contribute to insulin resistance, hindering ketosis.

Opening up Detox Pathways to Improve Weight Loss

To accelerate weight loss during fasting, keep your detox pathways open. Weight gain while fasting may be due to congested detox pathways, such as the liver, gut, kidneys, lymph, and skin. Ensure daily bowel movements, sweat regularly, stay hydrated, dry brush or loofah your skin, use castor oil packs over your liver, and get lymphatic drainage massage to prevent toxins from being stored in fat.

Preventing Unwanted Cycle Changes

Low progesterone can lead to spotting and missed menstrual cycles. Postmenopausal women may experience spotting after starting fasting, which is usually a sign of healing. Perimenopausal women with irregular cycles can use the 30-Day Fasting Reset to help regulate their cycles and alleviate menopause symptoms. Following fasting principles can have positive effects on hormonal balance and menstrual regularity.

Fasting and Specific Conditions

Fasting and Hair Loss

Hair loss can often be avoided by ensuring you have adequate mineral intake. Taking a mineral supplement can help promote hair growth. Additionally, varying fasting lengths and avoiding fasts longer If you are experiencing persistent hair loss despite trying mineral supplements and varying fasting lengths, consider getting a heavy metal test. Heavy metals like lead, mercury, and thallium can disrupt mineral absorption and contribute to hair loss. Additionally, be cautious about the chemicals in breast implants, as they may contain heavy metals. Removing implants can lead to improved health for some women experiencing hair loss. Avoiding fasting for more than 17 hours can prevent excessive toxin release that may contribute to hair loss.

Fasting and Fatigue

During your fasting journey, it's essential to understand that you are repairing your mitochondria, which may initially lead to fatigue. Allow yourself to rest and take power naps when needed. If low energy persists, consider using biohacking tools like red light therapy or a hyperbaric oxygen chamber to support your mitochondria. If fatigue persists for an extended period, consider detoxing to remove environmental toxins that may be affecting mitochondrial function.

Fasting and Medications

When it comes to medications and fasting, it's essential to consult your doctor as all medications may respond differently during fasting. Particularly, thyroid medication may have unique effects during fasting, such as increased sensitivity or heart rate changes. It is advisable to take thyroid medication during your eating window or with buttered coffee in the morning. Always communicate with your doctor about your fasting practices and discuss any necessary adaptations to your medication schedule.

Fasting and Supplements

In general, you can take your supplements during your fasting window, but it's a matter of personal preference. If you can tolerate supplements on an empty stomach, go ahead. However, if they cause nausea, consider taking them during your eating window instead. Avoid taking supplements during a three-day water fast, as it's best to let your body's natural healing processes occur without interference.

Fasting and Sleep

Some fasters may experience reduced sleep needs when incorporating fasting into their routine, especially with longer fasts. This is because both fasting and sleep are healing states, and the body may require less sleep to perform repair processes during fasting. Embrace this change and use early morning hours for journaling, meditation, or reading.

During longer fasts like three-day water fasts, some women may experience aches and pains, especially in the pelvic and low-back areas, as stem cells repair damaged tissues, including scar tissue from previous pregnancies. To ease this pain, consider increasing magnesium intake before bed to relax muscles and improve sleep quality. Additionally, try using CBD lotion or tincture to alleviate pain without side effects.

Fasting and Exercise

During shorter fasts, working out in a fasted state can be beneficial for weight loss. Exercising while fasting can lead to elevated blood sugar levels, and the body may metabolize fat more efficiently during these workouts. After the workout, breaking the fast with protein can help achieve a lean, muscular look.

However, during a three-day water fast, it's best to avoid exercising. This type of fast triggers a massive repair state in the body, similar to a healing state when having a fever. Halting all exercise during this fast allows the body to focus on complete repair and healing.

Fasting with a Thyroid Condition

Your thyroid's proper functioning involves five organs: the brain, thyroid, liver, gut, and adrenals. The process begins with the brain releasing TSH, which activates the thyroid to produce T4. T4 then converts to the bioactive T3 hormone in the liver and gut. However, adrenal fatigue can lead to elevated cortisol levels, resulting in the production of reverse T3, which is not useful for the cells. To ensure optimal thyroid function, it is crucial to address the health of these organs and reduce toxins and inflammation in the body.

Furthermore, fasting can improve thyroid health by promoting the repair of neurons in the brain, which is crucial for proper TSH production and hormonal communication. Fasting for 24 hours or more can also support gut healing, aiding in the conversion of T4 to the active T3 form. Additionally, fasting helps lower glucose levels, prompting the release of stored sugar from the liver, which facilitates the conversion of T4 to T3.

Contrary to some misconceptions, fasting does not permanently lower thyroid hormones. While there may be a temporary reduction in T3 during fasting, studies have shown that these effects are short-lived. After refeeding, T3 levels return to normal and, in some cases, may even increase beyond pre-fast levels.

Overall, fasting can have numerous benefits for thyroid function and hormone utilization. However, it's important to approach fasting mindfully, especially if you have a thyroid condition or are on thyroid medication. Consulting with a healthcare professional and monitoring your thyroid health during fasting is essential for optimal results.

Fasting with Adrenal Fatigue

Successfully fasting with adrenal fatigue requires a gradual approach, slowly increasing fasting windows over time to avoid excessive stress on the adrenals. Incorporating small amounts of hormetic stress can aid in adrenal repair, but it's essential not to push the adrenals too hard.

To support the adrenals during fasting, stabilizing blood sugar is crucial. Including plenty of healthy fats in the diet can help maintain stable blood sugar levels, making fasting easier on the adrenals.

It's important to recognize that adrenal fatigue involves more than just the adrenals. Seeking support from a functional practitioner who understands adrenal health can be beneficial for navigating the fasting process and optimizing overall health.

Fasting and Pregnancy and Breastfeeding

Do not fast if you are pregnant or breastfeeding.

Fasting and Diabetes

Both type 1 and type 2 diabetics can benefit from fasting, but caution is advised, especially for severe cases. It's recommended to work with a health practitioner and monitor blood sugar levels under supervision. If your doctor is unfamiliar with fasting, share the meta-analysis from The New England Journal of Medicine to help them understand the benefits.

Fasting and Eating Disorders

Individuals with a history of eating disorders should involve a doctor in their fasting journey to ensure safety and avoid dangerous mental paths.

Appendix: Fasting Protocols to Help with Specific Conditions

Infertility

Insulin resistance is a major cause of infertility in women, affecting one out of every eight women in the modern world. A fasting lifestyle can be a crucial step in fixing insulin resistance and balancing sex hormones to address fertility issues effectively.

2-month fasting protocol for infertility

Month 1

- Days 1–3: 15 hours intermittent fasting (ketobiotic)
- Days 4–10: 17 hours autophagy fasting (ketobiotic)
- Days 11–15: 13 hours intermittent fasting (hormone feasting)
- Days 16–19: 13 hours intermittent fasting (ketobiotic)
- Day 20–bleed (through day 28): no fasting (hormone feasting)

Month 2

- Days 1–5: 17 hours autophagy fasting (ketobiotic)
- Day 6: 24 hours gut-reset fast (ketobiotic)
- Days 7–10: 17 hours autophagy fasting (ketobiotic)
- Days 11–15: 13 hours intermittent fasting (hormone feasting)
- Day 16–bleed: no fasting (hormone feasting)

Autoimmune disorders

To address autoimmune conditions, focus on healing your gut and reducing toxic load through fasting. Incorporate gut reset (24 hours) and autophagy (17 hours) fasts into your monthly fasting regime. Prioritize the 30-Day Fasting Reset before attempting the advanced autoimmune protocol if needed.

Fasting protocol for autoimmunity

- Days 1–5: 17 hours autophagy fasting (ketobiotic)
- Days 6–7: 24 hours gut-reset fast (ketobiotic)
- Days 8–10: 17 hours autophagy fast (ketobiotic)
- Days 11–15: 15 hours intermittent fasting (hormone feasting)
- Days 16–17: 24 hours gut-reset fast (ketobiotic)
- Days 18–19: 17 hours autophagy fasting (ketobiotic)
- Day 20–bleed: 13 hours intermittent fasting (hormone feasting)

Thyroid conditions

For a fasting lifestyle that supports thyroid health, consider the interconnectedness of organs like the brain, liver, and gut. Prioritize autophagy fasting for thyroid conditions and incorporate hormone feasting foods with cruciferous and bitter greens to support the liver.

Fasting protocol for thyroid conditions

- Days 1–5: 15 hours intermittent fasting (ketobiotic)
- Days 6–8: 17 hours autophagy fasting (ketobiotic)
- Days 9–10: 24 hours gut-reset fast (ketobiotic)
- Days 11–15: 15 hours intermittent fasting (hormone feasting foods)
- Days 16–19: 17 hours autophagy fasting (ketobiotic)
- Day 20–bleed: 13 hours intermittent fasting (hormone feasting)

Chronic fatigue

Chronic fatigue can have multiple causes, with depleted cellular mitochondria, adrenal exhaustion, and Epstein-Barr virus being the most common. The protocol provided includes fasting, ketones, and a low-carb diet to address these root causes and support healing.

Fasting protocols for chronic fatigue

- Days 1–3: 13 hours intermittent fasting (ketobiotic)
- Days 4–6: 15 hours intermittent fasting (ketobiotic)
- Day 7: 17 hours autophagy fasting (ketobiotic)
- Days 8–9: 15 hours intermittent fasting (ketobiotic)
- Days 10–15: 13 hours intermittent fasting (hormone feasting foods)
- Days 16–19: 15 hours intermittent fasting (ketobiotic)
- Day 20–bleed: no fasting (hormone feasting)

Type 2 diabetes

For diabetics building a fasting lifestyle, involving your doctor is crucial. The root cause of type 2 diabetes is insulin resistance, and the fasting protocol aims to spend more time as a fat burner, monitoring blood sugar and insulin levels. The plan excludes a hormone-building day initially, focusing on stabilizing blood sugar before considering any changes and involving your doctor throughout the process.

Fasting protocol for type 2 diabetes

- Days 1–5: 13 hours intermittent fasting (ketobiotic)
- Days 6–10: 15 hours intermittent fasting (ketobiotic)
- Days 11–15: 13 hours intermittent fasting (hormone feasting)
- Day 16: 17 hours autophagy fasting (ketobiotic)
- Days 17–19: 13 hours intermittent fasting (ketobiotic)
- Day 20–bleed: no fasting (hormone feasting)

Brain health: memory loss, anxiety and depression

A fasting lifestyle can benefit memory issues and brain health by managing insulin and addressing heavy metal toxicity. Fasting helps improve insulin sensitivity and promotes the production of ketones, which are healing to the brain. The protocol includes autophagy fasting, focusing on fat-burning, and increasing mineral supplementation to support brain health and mood disorders like depression and anxiety.

Fasting protocol for memory loss

- Days 1–5: 17 hours autophagy fasting
- Days 6–7: 48 hours dopamine fasting
- Days 8–10: 15 hours intermittent fasting
- Days 11–15: 13 hours intermittent fasting
- Days 16–19: 17 hours autophagy fasting
- Day 20–bleed: 13 hours intermittent fasting

Adrenal fatigue

For those with adrenal fatigue, ease into fasting slowly and pay attention to the timing of each fast. Increase consumption of healthy fats to stabilize blood sugar and make fasting easier. Avoid a high-carbohydrate, low-fat diet, as it can make fasting difficult for those with adrenal fatigue.

Fasting protocol for adrenal fatigue

- Days 1–10: 10 hours intermittent fasting (pre-reset)
- Days 11–15: no fasting (hormone feasting)
- Days 16–19: 13 hours intermittent fasting (pre-reset)
- Days 20–28: no fasting (hormone feasting foods)

Immune system

For a serious immune system reset, opt for a three-day water fast during a power phase, monitoring blood sugar and ketone levels. Alternatively, incorporate autophagy fasting to enhance cell efficiency and pathogen-killing capabilities, especially if experiencing frequent colds or concerned about viruses.

Fasting protocol for immune system reset

- Days 1–5: 17 hours autophagy fasting (ketobiotic)
- Days 6–9: 72 hours three-day water fast
- Day 10: break water fast with four-step process
- Days 11–15: 17 hours autophagy fasting (ketobiotic)
- Days 16–18: 24 hours gut-reset fast (ketobiotic)
- Day 19–bleed: 15 hours intermittent fasting (hormone feasting)

30 Day Fasting Reset

Two Week Pre-Reset
Inexperienced fasters can use this time to prepare their bodies for the 30 day fasting reset

Foods to avoid:

Partially hydrogenated oils	Bread	Artificial Flavors and Colors
Corn oil	Pastas	Red or blue dyes
Cottonseed oil	Crackers	Saccharin
Canola oil	Desserts	NutraSweet
Vegetable oil		Splenda
Soybean oil		
Safflower oil		
Sunflower oil		

Foods to add:

Olive oil	Grass-fed beef
Avocado Oil	Bison
MCT oil	Turkey
Flaxseed oil	Chicken
Nut butters	Pork
Olives	Eggs
Avocados	Charcuterie meats

> ## Tips for a succesful reset:
>
> • Remove tempting food from your home
>
> • Surround yourself with people who support you
>
> • Plan your reset ahead of time—avoid months with lots of vacation, weddings, etc.

Tracking your progress

Day 1	Time	What I ate	
Breakfast			
Lunch			
Dinner			
Blood Sugar:		Ketones:	Hrs of sleep:

Day 2	Time	What I ate	
Breakfast			
Lunch			
Dinner			
Blood Sugar:		Ketones:	Hrs of sleep:

Day 3	Time	What I ate	
Breakfast			
Lunch			
Dinner			
Blood Sugar:		Ketones:	Hrs of sleep:

Day 4	Time	What I ate	
Breakfast			
Lunch			
Dinner			
Blood Sugar:		Ketones:	Hrs of sleep:

Day 5	Time	What I ate	
Breakfast			
Lunch			
Dinner			
Blood Sugar:		Ketones:	Hrs of sleep:

Day 6	Time	What I ate	
Breakfast			
Lunch			
Dinner			
Blood Sugar:		Ketones:	Hrs of sleep:

Day 7	Time	What I ate	
Breakfast			
Lunch			
Dinner			
Blood Sugar:		Ketones:	Hrs of sleep:

Day 8	Time	What I ate	
Breakfast			
Lunch			
Dinner			
Blood Sugar:		Ketones:	Hrs of sleep:

Day 9	Time	What I ate
Breakfast		
Lunch		
Dinner		
Blood Sugar:	Ketones:	Hrs of sleep:

Day 10	Time	What I ate
Breakfast		
Lunch		
Dinner		
Blood Sugar:	Ketones:	Hrs of sleep:

Day 11	Time	What I ate
Breakfast		
Lunch		
Dinner		
Blood Sugar:	Ketones:	Hrs of sleep:

Day 12	Time	What I ate
Breakfast		
Lunch		
Dinner		
Blood Sugar:	Ketones:	Hrs of sleep:

Day 13	Time	What I ate
Breakfast		
Lunch		
Dinner		
Blood Sugar:	Ketones:	Hrs of sleep:

Day 14	Time	What I ate
Breakfast		
Lunch		
Dinner		
Blood Sugar:	Ketones:	Hrs of sleep:

30 Day Fasting Reset

Now that you have finished the two week pre reset, you are ready for the 30 day fasting reset!

What to avoid during the reset:
Bad oils
Refined flour and sugar
Toxic Chemicals and ingredients
Alcohol

Power Phase One

Focus on eating ketobiotic foods
Day 1-4 Intermittent fasting (13 hours)
Day 5 Intermittent fasting (15 hours)
Day 6-10 Autophagy fasting (17 hours)

Day 1	Time	What I ate	
Breakfast			
Lunch			
Dinner			
Blood Sugar:		Ketones:	Hrs of sleep:

13 hours

Day 2	Time	What I ate	
Breakfast			
Lunch			
Dinner			
Blood Sugar:		Ketones:	Hrs of sleep:

13 hours

Day 3	Time	What I ate
Breakfast		
Lunch		
Dinner		
Blood Sugar:	Ketones:	Hrs of sleep:

13 hours

Day 4	Time	What I ate
Breakfast		
Lunch		
Dinner		
Blood Sugar:	Ketones:	Hrs of sleep:

13 hours

Day 5	Time	What I ate
Breakfast		
Lunch		
Dinner		
Blood Sugar:	Ketones:	Hrs of sleep:

15 hours

Day 6	Time	What I ate
Breakfast		
Lunch		
Dinner		
Blood Sugar:	Ketones:	Hrs of sleep:

17 hours

Day 7	Time	What I ate
Breakfast		
Lunch		
Dinner		
Blood Sugar:	Ketones:	Hrs of sleep:

17 hours

Day 8	Time	What I ate
Breakfast		
Lunch		
Dinner		
Blood Sugar:	Ketones:	Hrs of sleep:

17 hours

Day 9	Time	What I ate
Breakfast		
Lunch		
Dinner		
Blood Sugar:	Ketones:	Hrs of sleep:

17 hours

Day 10	Time	What I ate
Breakfast		
Lunch		
Dinner		
Blood Sugar:	Ketones:	Hrs of sleep:

17 hours

Manifestation Phase

Focus on eating hormone feasting foods
Day 11-15 Intermittent fasting (13 hours)

Day 11	Time	What I ate
Breakfast		
Lunch		
Dinner		
Blood Sugar:	Ketones:	Hrs of sleep:

13 hours

Day 12	Time	What I ate
Breakfast		
Lunch		
Dinner		
Blood Sugar:	Ketones:	Hrs of sleep:

13 hours

Day 13	Time	What I ate
Breakfast		
Lunch		
Dinner		
Blood Sugar:	Ketones:	Hrs of sleep:

13 hours

Day 14	Time	What I ate	
Breakfast			
Lunch			
Dinner			
Blood Sugar:		Ketones:	Hrs of sleep:

13 hours

Day 15	Time	What I ate	
Breakfast			
Lunch			
Dinner			
Blood Sugar:		Ketones:	Hrs of sleep:

13 hours

Power Phase 2

Focus on eating ketobiotic foods
Day 16-19 Intermittent fasting (15 hours)

Day 16	Time	What I ate	
Breakfast			
Lunch			
Dinner			
Blood Sugar:		Ketones:	Hrs of sleep:

15 hours

Day 17	Time	What I ate
Breakfast		
Lunch		
Dinner		
Blood Sugar:	Ketones:	Hrs of sleep:

15 hours

Day 18	Time	What I ate
Breakfast		
Lunch		
Dinner		
Blood Sugar:	Ketones:	Hrs of sleep:

15 hours

Day 19	Time	What I ate
Breakfast		
Lunch		
Dinner		
Blood Sugar:	Ketones:	Hrs of sleep:

15 hours

Nurture Phase

Focus on eating hormone feasting foods
Day 20-30 No fasting

Day 20	Time	What I ate
Breakfast		
Lunch		
Dinner		
Blood Sugar:	Ketones:	Hrs of sleep:

No fasting

Day 21	Time	What I ate
Breakfast		
Lunch		
Dinner		
Blood Sugar:	Ketones:	Hrs of sleep:

No fasting

Day 22	Time	What I ate
Breakfast		
Lunch		
Dinner		
Blood Sugar:	Ketones:	Hrs of sleep:

No fasting

Day 23	Time	What I ate
Breakfast		
Lunch		
Dinner		
Blood Sugar:	Ketones:	Hrs of sleep:

No fasting

Day 24	Time	What I ate
Breakfast		
Lunch		
Dinner		
Blood Sugar:	Ketones:	Hrs of sleep:

No fasting

Day 25	Time	What I ate
Breakfast		
Lunch		
Dinner		
Blood Sugar:	Ketones:	Hrs of sleep:

No fasting

Day 26	Time	What I ate	
Breakfast			
Lunch			
Dinner			
Blood Sugar:		Ketones:	Hrs of sleep:

No fasting

Day 27	Time	What I ate	
Breakfast			
Lunch			
Dinner			
Blood Sugar:		Ketones:	Hrs of sleep:

No fasting

Day 28	Time	What I ate	
Breakfast			
Lunch			
Dinner			
Blood Sugar:		Ketones:	Hrs of sleep:

No fasting

Day 29	Time	What I ate
Breakfast		
Lunch		
Dinner		
Blood Sugar:	Ketones:	Hrs of sleep:

No fasting

Day 30	Time	What I ate
Breakfast		
Lunch		
Dinner		
Blood Sugar:	Ketones:	Hrs of sleep:

No fasting

Advanced 30 Day Fasting

If you already have experience fasting, try this advanced 30 day fasting protocol.

What to avoid during the reset:

Bad oils
Refined flour and sugar
Toxic Chemicals and ingredients
Alcohol

Power Phase One

Focus on eating ketobiotic foods
Day 1-4 Intermittent fasting (15 hours)
Day 5 Gut reset (24 hours)
Day 6-10 Autophagy fasting (17 hours)

Day 1	Time	What I ate
Breakfast		
Lunch		
Dinner		
Blood Sugar:	Ketones:	Hrs of sleep:

15 hours

Day 2	Time	What I ate
Breakfast		
Lunch		
Dinner		
Blood Sugar:	Ketones:	Hrs of sleep:

15 hours

Day 3	Time	What I ate
Breakfast		
Lunch		
Dinner		
Blood Sugar:	Ketones:	Hrs of sleep:

15 hours

Day 4	Time	What I ate
Breakfast		
Lunch		
Dinner		
Blood Sugar:	Ketones:	Hrs of sleep:

15 hours

Day 5	Time	What I ate
Breakfast		
Lunch		
Dinner		
Blood Sugar:	Ketones:	Hrs of sleep:

24 hours

Day 6	Time	What I ate
Breakfast		
Lunch		
Dinner		
Blood Sugar:	Ketones:	Hrs of sleep:

17 hours

Day 7	Time	What I ate
Breakfast		
Lunch		
Dinner		
Blood Sugar:	Ketones:	Hrs of sleep:

17 hours

Day 8	Time	What I ate
Breakfast		
Lunch		
Dinner		
Blood Sugar:	Ketones:	Hrs of sleep:

17 hours

Day 9	Time	What I ate
Breakfast		
Lunch		
Dinner		
Blood Sugar:	Ketones:	Hrs of sleep:

17 hours

Day 10	Time	What I ate
Breakfast		
Lunch		
Dinner		
Blood Sugar:	Ketones:	Hrs of sleep:

17 hours

Manifestation Phase

Focus on eating hormone feasting foods
Day 11-15 Intermittent fasting (15 hours)

Day 11	Time	What I ate
Breakfast		
Lunch		
Dinner		
Blood Sugar:	Ketones:	Hrs of sleep:

15 hours

Day 12	Time	What I ate
Breakfast		
Lunch		
Dinner		
Blood Sugar:	Ketones:	Hrs of sleep:

15 hours

Day 13	Time	What I ate
Breakfast		
Lunch		
Dinner		
Blood Sugar:	Ketones:	Hrs of sleep:

15 hours

Day 14	Time	What I ate
Breakfast		
Lunch		
Dinner		
Blood Sugar:	Ketones:	Hrs of sleep:

13 hours

Day 15	Time	What I ate
Breakfast		
Lunch		
Dinner		
Blood Sugar:	Ketones:	Hrs of sleep:

13 hours

Power Phase 2

Focus on eating ketobiotic foods
Day 16 Gut reset (24 hours)
Day 17-19 Autophagy fasting (17 hours)

Day 16	Time	What I ate
Breakfast		
Lunch		
Dinner		
Blood Sugar:	Ketones:	Hrs of sleep:

24 hours

Day 17	Time	What I ate
Breakfast		
Lunch		
Dinner		
Blood Sugar:	Ketones:	Hrs of sleep:

17 hours

Day 18	Time	What I ate
Breakfast		
Lunch		
Dinner		
Blood Sugar:	Ketones:	Hrs of sleep:

17 hours

Day 19	Time	What I ate
Breakfast		
Lunch		
Dinner		
Blood Sugar:	Ketones:	Hrs of sleep:

17 hours

Nurture Phase

Focus on eating hormone feasting foods
Day 20-30 Intermittent fasting (13 hours)

Day 20	Time	What I ate	
Breakfast			
Lunch			
Dinner			
Blood Sugar:		Ketones:	Hrs of sleep:

13 Hours

Day 21	Time	What I ate	
Breakfast			
Lunch			
Dinner			
Blood Sugar:		Ketones:	Hrs of sleep:

13 Hours

Day 22	Time	What I ate	
Breakfast			
Lunch			
Dinner			
Blood Sugar:		Ketones:	Hrs of sleep:

13 Hours

Day 23	Time	What I ate
Breakfast		
Lunch		
Dinner		
Blood Sugar:	Ketones:	Hrs of sleep:

13 Hours

Day 24	Time	What I ate
Breakfast		
Lunch		
Dinner		
Blood Sugar:	Ketones:	Hrs of sleep:

13 Hours

Day 25	Time	What I ate
Breakfast		
Lunch		
Dinner		
Blood Sugar:	Ketones:	Hrs of sleep:

13 Hours

Day 26	Time	What I ate
Breakfast		
Lunch		
Dinner		
Blood Sugar:	Ketones:	Hrs of sleep:

13 Hours

Day 27	Time	What I ate
Breakfast		
Lunch		
Dinner		
Blood Sugar:	Ketones:	Hrs of sleep:

13 Hours

Day 28	Time	What I ate
Breakfast		
Lunch		
Dinner		
Blood Sugar:	Ketones:	Hrs of sleep:

13 Hours

Day 29	Time	What I ate
Breakfast		
Lunch		
Dinner		
Blood Sugar:	Ketones:	Hrs of sleep:

13 Hours

Day 30	Time	What I ate
Breakfast		
Lunch		
Dinner		
Blood Sugar:	Ketones:	Hrs of sleep:

13 Hours

Made in the USA
Coppell, TX
24 September 2023

21962379R00042